Narcissism

An In-Depth Manual For Comprehending The Origins Of Narcissism And Cultivating Resilience To Counteract Narcissistic Abuse, Toxic Codependency, And Manipulation

(Resources And Techniques For Healing From Abuse, Recovering, And Building Resilience)

Dwayne FitzGerald

TABLE OF CONTENT

Acknowledging Narcissistic Features........................... 1

Comprehending The Narcissistic World 13

Recognizing The Traits Of A Narcissist....................... 29

Clinical Terms And Standards 42

Exposing Narcissistic Maltreatment 66

Promoting Acceptance Of Oneself: 98

Phases Of Drug Addiction... 115

Narcissistic Personality Disorder Causes 136

When It's Convenient For Them, They Will Speak.
.... 161

Acknowledging Narcissistic Features

This chapter expands on our knowledge of narcissism by exploring the characteristics and warning indicators of selfish people. By recognizing these characteristics, readers can learn important tips for spotting narcissism in various contexts, including work and personal relationships. We demonstrate the variety of ways that narcissistic tendencies can appear through case studies and real-world examples, giving readers the information they need to recognize and negotiate these intricate interactions.

Charm and charisma are often masks for narcissism, which can be misleading. By delving into the subtleties of narcissistic conduct, we provide readers with the means to discern between constructive narcissism and healthy self-assurance. Setting limits and promoting healthy relationships begin with identifying these characteristics.

NARCISSISM'S IMPACT ON RELATIONSHIPS

The complex interactions between narcissism and relationships are examined in this chapter. Narcissistic characteristics can have a significant impact on relationships, whether they are romantic, familial, or friendship-based. These relationships are frequently characterized by conflict, manipulation, and emotional pain. We look at the emotional cost of being in a narcissistic relationship and offer advice on how to deal with these difficulties.

We analyze the dynamics of narcissistic relationships, from the idealization cycle to the devaluation cycle. Readers will learn more about the emotional rollercoaster that people who are close to narcissistic people frequently go through. This chapter also provides helpful advice on how to manage the intricacies of narcissistic relationships while maintaining one's mental and emotional well.

Identifying Narcissistic Patterns in Your Partnership

Indices of Partner Narcissistic Behavior

The first step in resolving toxic dynamics in a relationship is identifying narcissistic conduct in a partner. In this subchapter, we will look at common indicators of selfish behaviour in marriages. Couples can create coping mechanisms to deal with the difficulties of cohabitating with a narcissistic partner by being aware of these symptoms.

An overwhelming desire for recognition and attention is one of the main indicators of narcissistic conduct. A spouse with narcissism may be continuously looking for approval and recognition, frequently at the expense of others. They could act arrogant, thinking they are entitled to preferential treatment and benefits. As a result, they could minimize or disregard their partner's needs and emotions.

It might be difficult for a partner of a selfish person to feel understood and supported since narcissistic people frequently find it difficult to comprehend or value the emotions of others. To keep control of the relationship, they could also play on their partner's feelings by assigning blame or feelings of guilt.

Narcissistic spouses frequently exhibit haughty and grandiose behaviour and excessive feelings of self-importance. They might always try to steal the show, taking over talks and discounting other people's viewpoints. This may result in a power imbalance and a lack of respect for one another in the relationship.

Furthermore, gaslighting is a manipulative technique used by narcissistic partners to cause their partners to question their reality and perceptions. Their spouse might start to doubt their memory or sanity if they reject or misrepresent historical occurrences. The victim of gaslighting may become more reliant on their narcissistic spouse and see their self-esteem decline.

To safeguard their mental health, couples who live with a narcissistic partner should learn coping mechanisms. This could entail establishing clear limits, taking care of oneself, and asking for help from dependable family members, friends, or experts. Couples counselling is another helpful resource for couples. It may guide them through the difficulties posed by a narcissistic spouse and help them develop more positive relationship dynamics.

By identifying selfish behaviour in a partner and applying coping mechanisms, couples can initiate the process of addressing and resolving the toxic dynamics in their relationship. It is important to keep in mind that the person exhibiting narcissistic qualities is ultimately responsible for bringing about change. However, couples can find empowerment and support in working through these issues together.

Recognizing the Narcissistic Abuse Cycle
You may feel helpless, alone, and bewildered as a result of the ongoing emotional abuse, gaslighting, and manipulation.

Phases one through three of the narcissistic abuse cycle are idealization, devaluation, and discard. The narcissist puts up an attractive and captivating persona to win you over during the idealization phase. They treat you like the most important person in their life by showing you so much love, care, and appreciation. This stage fosters an emotional connection and euphoria, making it difficult to see the warning flags.

But as the relationship develops, throughout the devaluation stage, the narcissist's true nature becomes apparent. They can start acting rudely, critically, and emotionally aloof. They influence your emotions, minimize your accomplishments, and diminish your value. This stage will undermine your self-worth and make you reliant on their acceptance.

The narcissist moves into the discard phase as soon as they believe they have control over you. This is when people break up with each other suddenly or emotionally remove themselves. They might begin to mistreat you, stop answering your calls, or even cancel plans. This stage is designed to control and dominate you, making you feel helpless and in need of their attention.

It's critical to keep in mind that unless you end the cycle of abuse, it will not end.

Setting and maintaining boundaries is one coping mechanism. Establishing boundaries with others might help you preserve your sense of self and safeguard your mental health since narcissists enjoy dominating others. Seek assistance from dependable family members, friends, or therapists who can offer a secure setting to communicate your emotions and obtain perspective.

It's also critical to prioritize taking care of yourself. Take part in things that make you happy and increase your worth. Take up hobbies, engage in mindfulness exercises, and be in the company of positive people. You may regain control of your life and develop resilience by putting your well-being first.

In conclusion, couples dealing with a narcissistic partner must comprehend the cycle of narcissistic abuse. People can proactively safeguard themselves by identifying the processes of idealization, devaluation, and disposal. Setting limits, getting help, and putting self-care first are crucial coping mechanisms for escaping the destructive dynamics of a narcissistic relationship. Never forget that you deserve to be in a loving, healthy relationship free from abuse.

Comprehending The Narcissistic World

1.1 Narcissism Definition: Going Beyond Vanity

Do you believe you understand what narcissism is, then? Do you think it's another word for conceit, overindulgence in oneself, or the unbridled ego we frequently witness in showy celebrities? The narrative above is not as simple as it seems. There is more to narcissism than merely an infatuation with one's reflection or a preference for self-indulgent monologues. Let's clarify this frequently misinterpreted term.

Fundamentals of Narcissism

Narcissism is, by definition, a pattern of conduct characterized by a strong self-centeredness, a strong desire for approval and affection, and a marked lack of real empathy for other people. The Greek myth of Narcissus, whose obsession with introspection ultimately led to his demise, is where the term "narcissism" first appeared. Even while this story presents a vivid image, true narcissism goes beyond excessive self-love.

Each day, In contrast to narcissistic personality disorder, narcissism

Yes, everyone occasionally exhibits narcissistic traits. It is typical to develop an obsession with one's achievements, approval from others, and self-love. One is not classified as a narcissist by this. It's human nature to occasionally take pride in our accomplishments and seek approval.

Yet, a more potent and persistent pattern is Narcissistic Personality Disorder (NPD). An exaggerated sense of self-importance, a pervasive need for excessive praise and attention, strained interpersonal interactions, and a glaring lack of empathy for others are all characteristics of NPD patients.

The Fallacy About Absolute Vanity.

It's simple to confuse pure vanity with narcissism. After all, an obsession with oneself is a prevalent characteristic of narcissism. But it's crucial to realize that narcissism is more than just having a high self-esteem or outward appearance. A weak sense of who they are, an impending fear of being criticized, and an underlying weakness that they strongly defend are the core causes of narcissistic behaviour.

The boundaries separating narcissism might be hazy in the digital environment we live in. The explosion of social media has made self-promotion commonplace. But keep in mind that posting a selfie or acknowledging one's accomplishments on social media does not always indicate narcissism. It concerns the motivation behind the deed and the emotional reliance on these kinds of confirmations.

Narcissism: Overt vs. Covert

Not every narcissist is made equal. In addition to the 'overt' narcissist who is always seeking attention and compliments, there is also the 'covert' narcissist who is more reserved and less visible. Hypersensitivity, passive hostility, and victimization are signs of this narcissistic state. While they might not be the centre of attention in every conversation, they nevertheless project an unjustified sense of superiority and lack of empathy.

The Importance of Establishing Actual Narcissism

It can be harmful to incorrectly diagnose someone as narcissistic or to misread narcissistic tendencies. Good knowledge of narcissism is important, whether one is trying to understand oneself, others, or the workplace.

Understanding the subtleties of narcissism is the first step toward establishing healthy boundaries, getting help if necessary, and managing relationships with people who display these characteristics. Recognizing the underlying motives and patterns is important rather than placing blame or applying labels.

We'll learn more about this branch and the causes of narcissistic behaviour. Whether it is a product of nature or nurture is the question. Or maybe a mix of the two? We'll also discuss the differences between narcissism and healthy self-esteem. Despite their apparent similarities, they have quite diverse bases.

We shall also look at a narcissistic person's perspective. What motivates them? What worries them? Knowing this can help you better understand their actions and strategies for productive communication.

Lastly, we shall talk about the telltale signs of encountering a narcissist. Knowing these patterns, from the early warning signs to the more overt activities, can enable people to deal with prospective narcissists in a more informed and wise manner.

In conclusion, narcissism is a multifaceted concept with a range of abilities and expressions, even though it may appear obvious at first. This element serves as a foundation, offering a more thorough view of the narcissistic universe. This place imparts knowledge not only for comprehending others but also for self-reflection. One must possess comprehension to demonstrate empathy, progress, and communicate effectively.

1.2 Where Narcissistic Behavior Comes From

While delving into the realm of narcissism, you might wonder how someone might become narcissistic or perhaps develop a full-blown Narcissistic Personality Disorder. These behaviours have complicated roots, similar to the layers of an onion. To find the causes, let's explore these layers.

Is it Nature or Nurture? The Age-Old Argument

For a long time, researchers and psychologists have disagreed over whether conduct is more influenced by our surroundings and upbringing (nurture) or by our genetic composition (nature). The general agreement? It combines the two.

1) Genetic Predisposition: Research has indicated that narcissism may have hereditary roots. People who have narcissistic parents or relatives may be more likely to acquire these characteristics. But genetics does not

mean fate. They are but a piece of a larger jigsaw puzzle.

2) Early Childhood Environment: This is an important picture component. Narcissistic tendencies can emerge in children raised in circumstances where they receive either excessive praise or criticism. A child may develop a sense of entitlement if they receive praise all the time. On the other hand, if they experience constant denigration, they may acquire these characteristics as a bulwark against ingrained emotions of worthlessness.

Parenting's Function

We frequently undervalue the profound influence that parenting has on a person's psychological development.

Several parenting practices can foster the development of narcissistic behaviour:

1) Overvaluation: Narcissistic conduct can be unintentionally encouraged by parents who feel their kids are better than others and refuse to face their transgressions. Although it's normal for parents to think only positively of their kids, an imbalance might cause a child to develop an exaggerated sense of self.

2) Lack of Realistic Feedback: Preventing kids from experiencing reality and giving them unreal feedback can prepare them for difficulties. They could be frustrated by obstacles or criticism because they assume everyone would treat them similarly.

3) Conditional Love: Children may identify their value with accomplishments if love and appreciation are bestowed contingent upon them or on certain conditions, which may lead them to constantly seek affirmation.

Social Affects: Existing in the Age of "Me" Narcissistic habits have flourished because of the emphasis on personal accomplishments, celebrity culture, and social media platforms in modern culture. Many people get into the trap of confusing online attention with self-esteem when they believe that receiving "likes" indicates merit and affirmation.

The media frequently glamorizes the " self-made " person, prioritizing individual success over communal values. It is simple to understand how selfish attitudes might spread when society emphasizes individual achievement at the expense of empathy, compassion, or teamwork.

Events Traumatic and the Development of Defense Mechanisms

Narcissism can sometimes be the result of prior trauma. Adversity in a person's life, particularly in their formative years, might trigger the emergence of protective mechanisms, such as narcissistic conduct.

To restore control, a child who is bullied, for example, may inflate their sense of self as a protective shield, bragging about their accomplishments or demeaning others. It's important to understand that, at its core, narcissism frequently serves as a coping strategy, a technique to deal with underlying hurt and insecurity.

The Intricate Web of Narcissistic Roots

Though it can be tempting to identify a single component that leads to selfish behaviour, a combination of cultural circumstances, upbringing, genetics, and personal experiences is responsible. While knowing these roots doesn't justify harmful, selfish behaviour, it does provide a perspective that helps us understand and sympathize.

We will further differentiate between true self-esteem and narcissism in this chapter as we continue to explore the depths of narcissism. Although they may seem alike, these have quite different bases. We'll also take a deep dive into the turbulent inner world of narcissists, delving into their motivations, fears, and the internal turmoil that frequently rages.

To further equip ourselves with information and awareness, we'll also discuss the early warning indicators of a meeting with a narcissist. Establishing boundaries and protecting our emotional well-being begin with recognizing these warning indicators.

In summary, narcissistic behaviours have a variety of underlying causes. By gaining knowledge of these foundations, we equip ourselves with the knowledge necessary to direct our interactions with these people and create a healing and understanding environment. After all, gaining knowledge is the first step toward empowerment.

Recognizing The Traits Of A Narcissist

Up until now, you could have been unsure of whether you are in a relationship with a narcissist and may still be wondering. Recall that it is unhealthy to be in a relationship with someone who makes you feel unloved and unworthy, and your spouse may have narcissistic traits.

Never forget that millions worldwide are experiencing exactly what you are now and are not alone. I want to clarify a few things regarding how to recognize narcissist traits. Most people who are being abused by narcissists or who have survived narcissistic abuse have had to accept that they would need to make some difficult decisions to safeguard themselves from the abuse they have been subjected to.

Knowing how to spot a narcissist is an essential ability for anyone trying to comprehend the intricacies of interpersonal interactions and human behaviour. In this chapter, I'll go over the key characteristics that characterize narcissism and discuss the warning indicators that can help you identify this personality disorder.

Let us begin at the outset. The core of narcissistic personality traits is a deeply ingrained feeling of grandiosity. People who suffer from narcissism tend to have an exaggerated sense of their importance and ability due to this grandiose self-image. Narcissists believe they are unique and should receive particular attention; thus, they will always seek praise, affirmation, and preferential treatment. It is critical to recognize these characteristics by observing how these people habitually direct discourse toward their accomplishments, minimize the accomplishments of others or display an insatiable want for attention and validation.

One of the most recognizable traits of a narcissist is their inability to truly demonstrate empathy. In any kind of connection, a narcissist is frequently unable to understand or relate to the needs and feelings of others. This extends beyond romantic partnerships. It pertains to their friendships, job environment, and family interactions. They see people as extensions of themselves or tools, valued only to the extent that they can fulfil their needs. It is essential to identify how the person you are in a relationship with behaves or does not respond to emotional events, especially in stressful or vulnerable situations, to identify this trait.

It is common for narcissists to indulge in illusions of unending beauty, power, success, or perfect love. For them, these fantasies are essential to who they are and not just daydreams. They frequently display an obsession with idealized versions of themselves, which can lead them to act in ways that support their irrational views. Examples of these actions include rashly pursuing endeavours to establish their superiority or looking for validation on social media. Anything to project an illusion of grandeur, superiority, and accomplishment beyond what they possess.

Additionally, you might observe that the person you see uses deceptive and predatory tactics when interacting with others, counting on their charisma and charm to trick others into granting them what they want.

Everyone who knows you will believe your relationship is ideal from the outside looking in. You might even believe that you will be viewed negatively if you depart. Recall that it is your responsibility to liberate yourself from the toxic behaviours and emotional abuse you are experiencing and that other people's opinions about your circumstances are meaningless. These people do not have to deal with constant emotional upheaval. Indeed, you are!

The only time you can start acting in a way that will help you start to heal from your experiences is if you have thought about, recognized, and determined that you are in a narcissistic relationship. Without further ado, let's talk about how to spot a narcissist.

Absence of Compassion

Relationship dynamics with narcissists can be confusing and emotionally taxing. One of the most important and concerning aspects of narcissism is at the core of this complexity: a deep lack of empathy!

However, why? Why is empathy absent in narcissists? This question has a more nuanced answer than you might imagine. German researchers conducted a study in an attempt to understand why narcissists are not emotionally empathic. Researchers looking at brain scans from narcissistic individuals discovered that the brain regions thought to be connected to empathy have less brain matter than those without narcissistic tendencies. This indicates that they lack the brain function necessary for an individual to "feel" empathy on a very genuine and psychological level. It is a difficult idea to address.

There are various ways in which their lack of empathy shows up, and each one adds to the emotional burden that people who are in relationships with narcissists bear. The primary ways in which a narcissist lacks empathy are when they disregard your needs, assign blame to you for their mistakes, and dismiss your feelings.

Disregarding Your Emotions

A deep-seated sense of self-importance causes a narcissist's emotional detachment. Put another way, a narcissist is mainly focused on oneself, including their feelings, goals, and wants. There is frequently little opportunity for sincere concern or interest in the feelings of others because of this self-absorption.

A narcissist is unaware of who they are. They feel that everything about them is open to public viewing and that their lives are a performance, a theatrical work of art. They don't give their loved ones any room to connect with them since, to them, the show must go on!

Let's take the scenario when you are thrilled with a personal victory. Narcissists will immediately change the subject to their successes, ignoring your emotions.

It is well-recognized that narcissists are ill-suited to invalidate the emotions of others around them. When faced with feelings or concerns, they typically dismiss them as unimportant, unreasonable, or unjustified. Due to this invalidation, Others will question the validity of their feelings. Assume that you are expressing your sorrow over a personal loss. In response, a narcissist frequently says something dismissive, such as, "Why are you making such a big deal out of it? It isn't very significant.

Have you ever remembered a cruel remark a narcissist said to you? Did they vehemently deny ever saying anything when you challenged them, making you doubt your recollection and reality? This deceptive strategy, "gaslighting," is designed to cause people to question their reality. A narcissist will twist events, deny their words or deeds, or even accuse others of creating problems they never caused. Their way of living is a true embodiment of the phrase "deny till you die."

Comprehending the reasons behind a narcissist's indifference to emotions is intricate and frequently stems from their character attributes and mental constitution. Put simply, narcissists frequently experience deep disappointment when they do not receive the particular attention or unwavering praise they believe they are entitled to.

We've already discussed how dating a narcissist can make you feel as though you're in a soap opera. This is because they frequently discover that their relationships are empty. Therefore, they feed off of the turmoil they bring into the lives of their partners. They feel more significant the more drama they create. They want to be the solution to the issue that they brought about for you.

It may not always be obvious, but you are most likely in an unhealthy, emotionally abusive, and toxic relationship if your partner has an exaggerated feeling of self-importance and a persistent need for approval and affirmation.

Because they cannot completely comprehend the emotional consequences of their activities, they frequently fail to notice when their actions have injured someone emotionally. This limited empathy also makes it difficult for them to connect with or acknowledge the feelings of others around them.

You will try your hardest to express your sentiments to a narcissist in a relationship most understandably and succinctly possible, but they won't connect with it. They can't hear or comprehend you, making it seem like you speak a foreign language.

Clinical Terms And Standards

Imagine that you are putting together a jigsaw puzzle. The frame is formed by connecting the edge parts. A few groups of comparable hues and forms are dispersed across the table. Putting everything together is thrilling, but the puzzle isn't solved until you have the whole image. Comprehending narcissism can resemble trying to solve a very difficult riddle. We've discussed the myths, cultural perceptions, and all-too-deceptive notions of harmlessness surrounding this subject. Now, though, let's get down to business: what do experts say about narcissism?

The DSM-5 and the Details

A person needs to satisfy five out of nine criteria—which include grandiosity, a deficiency in empathy, and an intense desire for admiration—to be diagnosed with NPD. While knowing these standards can provide useful information, remember that diagnosing someone else is not your place.

Grandiosity: Beyond Self-Confusion

An overblown sense of grandiosity or self-importance is a fundamental feature of narcissism. But hold on, isn't self-esteem a necessary component for everyone? Yes, but there's a difference between grandiosity and self-worth. Grandiosity is the belief that one is better than others and should be treated differently, while self-esteem is recognizing and appreciating one's value. Grandiose people don't just run the marathon of life; they think they've already won and don't understand why anyone else is still out there.

The Imaginary World and the Need for Admiration

Here is a fantasy realm where narcissists, especially overt ones, love to reside. They are the kings or queens of their domain. Whether they are stay-at-home parents, Hollywood stars, or CEOs of large organizations, they all yearn for approval and affirmation. If you've ever complimented a narcissist, you may have observed how they soaked in the affirmation as water does. This is necessary for their self-esteem, not merely because they are flatterers at heart.

Changing Empathy: A Two-Way Process

We discussed earlier how empathy—or the absence of it—is a key component of narcissism. For the covert narcissist, this manifests as a selective type of empathy—being empathic when it suits them and coldly apathetic when it does not.

Relationships and Behavior that Exploit

The propensity of narcissists to be exploitative is another factor taken into account by clinicians. This is not to say that all narcissists are constantly plotting to control other people—though some probably are). It denotes a tendency on their part to use others as a tool for achieving goals they may have, such as elevating their social standing, advancing their careers, or exerting emotional control.

Feelings of Envy and Thinking Others Are Envious

When you tell someone they have excellent news, have you ever seen someone scowl as though they just ate a lemon? That could be your egotistical persona coming out. For many people with NPD, envy is a defining characteristic rather than just a quality. Their idea that other people are just as jealous of them is even more strange—they live in a society where most are rivals or fans, rarely just friends.

Unique vs. Special: The Elitist Perspective

To be fair, many of us like to think of ourselves as distinct individuals. A narcissist, on the other hand, goes beyond this. They believe that only other "special" or high-status individuals can fully comprehend them, not merely because they are unusual. Due to this thinking, they look for partnerships and circumstances where they may keep their enhanced status.

The Adaptable Self-Portrait

The weakness of narcissism is its paradox. Even with their ostentatious façade, many narcissists harbour a weak sense of who they are. They are very sensitive to criticism, and if they feel that their "grand" image is in danger, they may become angry, humiliated, or withdraw.

Is Covert Narcissism Diagnosis Possible?

The DSM-5's criteria are more specifically designed to diagnose overt narcissism, which makes identifying covert narcissism more difficult. Narcissists hiding under the guise of being modest, reserved, or self-deprecating can go unnoticed. While they're not as obvious, their fundamental characteristics—manipulation, a lack of empathy, and a desire for validation—remain the same.

This chapter delves deeper into the medical underbelly of narcissism, revealing a complex and diverse condition that affects not just the person with it but also those near them. As we go along, we'll discuss coping strategies, available treatments, and how to defend yourself if you find yourself trapped in a narcissist's web.

As one might expect, it takes more than just reading a list of symptoms to comprehend narcissism. It necessitates a thorough examination of the psychological processes involved. So, shall we continue assembling this complex puzzle?

Chapter 1: Introduction and Background

The term narcissism, which is both alluring and elusive, is profoundly ingrained in our culture. As a psychologist and sociologist, my work has led me into the maze of the human psyche, where the mystery of narcissism has often surfaced and called for reflection and comprehension. Many of the people who came through my door were burdened by this issue, either personally or as a difficulty in their interpersonal interactions.

A thorough examination of the wide field of narcissism is provided in this chapter. We'll investigate the historical background from which it originated, examine how it has shaped and been shaped by cultural contexts, and traverse the spectrum of narcissism to comprehend its myriad manifestations, ranging from constructive self-love that propels us forward to more maladaptive forms that can obstruct our interpersonal interactions and personal development.

Let's approach this chapter with an open mind, realizing that narcissism is a complicated interaction of personal experiences, psychology, culture, and history rather than just a term or label.

Overview of Narcissism

You've likely heard the word "narcissism" a lot—sometimes in informal talks, maybe even about you in different situations. Misunderstandings and oversimplifications frequently taint this phrase. I want you to know that you are brave for delving deeper into this and that we will work through its complexities together.

I've had the honour of interacting with several people throughout my years of experience, each with their own story. It's critical to realize that narcissism is a mindset and a particular manner of dealing with the outside world, not just about what is outwardly apparent. It has to do with the particular perspective you have on life.

Narcissism is fundamentally about one's connection with oneself. This is a multifaceted, intricate, and profound relationship. It concerns how someone feels about themselves, where they think they fit in the world, and how they get approval. However, it's critical to remember that this is a general label.

Because narcissism is a result of a person's life events, internal stories, and relationships with others, each person's experience with it is distinct. The details are what count, even though the outside world frequently portrays this in general terms.

I have direct experience with the immense potential that can be realized by comprehending and manipulating one's mentality, having participated in numerous life-changing experiences. This book is moulded by the observations and reflections gained from these trips, offering a path that recognizes, embraces, and plays to your strengths rather than attempting to change who you are at your core.

This exploration is not about you alone. Realizing your value, comprehending your feelings and thoughts, and striking a balance that promotes your development and wellbeing are all important. With an open mind and heart, let's dive into this exploration, knowing that self-awareness is the first step to significant change.

Cultural and Historical Background

It's really helpful to step back for a moment to completely understand the complexities of narcissism and how it manifests in your life. By delving into historical and cultural settings, we can better comprehend how this particular aspect of the human experience has been viewed, handled, and articulated across periods and societies.

The origins of narcissism can be found in old stories, particularly the fable of Narcissus. This young man became a symbol of deep introspection after becoming fascinated by his reflection in placid waters. However, his tale goes beyond a simple folktale of conceit. It reflects the age-old dance that humans have with their self-perception and the harmony between self-absorption and self-appreciation.

Different cultures and historical periods have contributed their viewpoints to this dance throughout history.

There have been times when people have embraced their individuality and allowed it to make them shine. In other periods, people were pushed to discover their position in the bigger picture by the priority of social harmony.

In today's dynamic environment, narcissism assumes various forms and subtleties. Our self-perception and search for affirmations of our value are shaped by the various platforms we access, ranging from literature and the arts to the extensive world of social media. These contemporary channels present many chances for self-expression but also difficulties. It's a dynamic dance between realizing one's inherent value and looking for validation.

The fact remains, nevertheless, that every culture and era has both strengths and weaknesses. Also, your journey is woven throughout this exquisite tapestry. As we go forward, remember that the objective is to comprehend the larger settings and derive conclusions consistent with your experiences rather than fitting a specific mould.

You're not the exception. Your thoughts and emotions are a part of the vast range of human experience. Gaining a comprehensive understanding of history and culture allows us to make insightful decisions about navigating both the personal and the contemporary. We will investigate, consider, and choose pathways that align with your journey to promote development, comprehension, and sincere self-appreciation.

Identifying Relationship Patterns of Narcissism

I

Recognizing the telltale symptoms of being caught in a narcissistic relationship pattern is essential to comprehending your circumstances and making plans. The following are some crucial signs to watch out for:

Love Bombing: A narcissistic partner may show you an excessive amount of love and attention in the early stages of the relationship. This relationship stage seems very personal and could see quick relationship development. You may be exalted and shown as the ideal companion. This early passion can last longer than other partnerships' customary honeymoon phases. This "love bombing" is meant to instil a sense of obligation in you, making you feel responsible for reciprocating to gain control.

Manipulation and Gaslighting: To exert control over other people and circumstances, narcissists frequently use manipulative techniques. These tactics, albeit not necessarily intentional, can be harmful to your mental health. Manipulation may include inciting feelings of guilt, envy, or even intimidation. Distorting your reality is the goal of emotional abuse, known as gaslighting. Your partner may overtly dispute activities they've performed, question your memory of events, or bring up prior mistakes that trigger you regularly. If you tell them how their actions affect your physical or mental wellbeing wellbeing, they may call you excessively sensitive and place the responsibility on you. Statements such as "You're overreacting," "That never happened," or "You need help" may be encountered.

Triangulation: Using a third party, frequently an ally, to support the narcissist's point of view during disputes is known as "triangulation" in the context of narcissistic relationship dynamics. This is a ploy to make you look foolish or guilty. Your spouse could turn to your former relationships, relatives, or friends to reinforce their position. They may use statements like "Your mother agrees with me" or "Your ex would say the same thing" to draw attention to themselves and put you in the back seat.

The Narcissistic Abuse Cycle:

In narcissistic relationships, abuse frequently occurs in a repeating cycle:

Love Bombing: You are idealized and put on a pedestal in the first phase, which makes you feel important and unique.

Devaluation: As the relationship develops, actual and imagined imperfections come to light. It's possible to start hearing criticism, humiliation, and low self-esteem frequently.

Rejection and Discarding: At this point, your lover can start to move away from you. Triangulation and gaslighting techniques may get more intense, equating you with a newly idealized figure they've introduced into the relationship.

4. Constantly boasting and talking about themselves:

Needing a lot of attention is a sign of narcissism. They find it difficult to let others shine and need attention. They're not confident inside; therefore, they require praise to feel good about themselves. This could be seen by your partner trying to make every conversation about them, complimenting them on everything, no matter how trivial, and making it seem like everything is all about them.

5. Refusing to Take Accounts:

It's difficult for narcissists to acknowledge their mistakes. It's difficult for them because they utilize their large egos to mask their lack of confidence. It terrifies people to be vulnerable when taking responsibility. Your partner may hold you accountable in your relationship for their mistakes. If you attempt to hold them responsible, they may fabricate tales to make you appear guilty and angry.

6. Absence of Emotional Closeness and Empathy:

Narcissists find it difficult to empathize with others. They presume that everyone feels the same way they do and view others as extensions of themselves. Should you feel differently, they may belittle you. When they damage your feelings, they don't seem to regret it.

7. Steer Clear of Conversations:

Your feelings in a relationship can reveal whether or not it's safe. Relationships with narcissists frequently feel uncomfortable. To avoid making them angry, you might tiptoe around conversations. You may be caught in a narcissistic pattern if you believe that talking to your partner will result in an argument where they won't listen, blame you for everything, and accept responsibility.

Recall that identifying these indicators might assist you in determining the next course of action and comprehending what is going on in your relationship.

Exposing Narcissistic Maltreatment

In many stories, the antagonist isn't always a terrifying person lurking in the background; instead, they can be friends, lovers, or confidants. Similar to this, narcissistic abuse is often concealed by charisma, compassion, or affection, which makes it even more sneaky and challenging to spot.

Qualities of a Narcissist

Recognizing and stopping abuse requires an understanding of the nuanced nature of a narcissist. A narcissist may display a variety of characteristics that distort your experience. These characteristics can be subtle yet have a big influence on relationships. Let's take a closer look:

Excessive Feeling of Personal Importance:

An exaggerated feeling of self-worth and an ego fed by an illusion of grandeur are common traits among narcissists. Without any evidence to support them, they might boast excessively about their accomplishments and claim to be better than others.

As an illustration:

When a spouse feels that they are smarter than you or more attractive than you are, they won't accept your success until it makes them look better.

A friend who dominates conversations and forces everyone to talk only about themselves, their accomplishments, and their experiences, giving little chance for others to participate or shine.

Dreams of Unending Fortune, Strength, Beauty, or Perfect Love:

Unrealistic dreams that put themselves first and frequently ignore the thoughts, feelings, and goals of others are held by narcissists.

As an illustration:

A workmate who conjures up stories about how they come from nothing to save the day or become extremely famous and who is always looking for approval for their dreams.

A partner who minimizes your wants and desires and expects you to fit into their romanticized picture of a relationship, believing they are entitled to perfect love and admiration.

Controlling or Manipulative Behavior: Narcissists frequently employ strategies like gaslighting, which trick you into doubting your own experiences and perceptions to exercise control over other people.

As an illustration:

By deceiving staff members into questioning their abilities, a manager fosters a reliance on their approval.

A manipulative partner that makes you walk on eggshells to avoid disagreement at all costs by framing events so that they are the victim?

The Narcissistic Abuse Cycle

The victim of narcissistic abuse is typically trapped in a predictable cycle of abuse that undermines their self-worth and encourages reliance. This cycle is divided by experts into stages of Idealization, Devaluation, and disposal, which combine to form an intricate web of control and manipulation:

The phase of Idealization:

The narcissist puts on a front of perfection throughout this stage and shows you love and appreciation. The first level of Idealization deceives you into thinking you are safe, which makes it hard to see when manipulation and control are about to occur.

As an illustration:

A new companion who presents themselves as your ideal counterpart reflects your goals and aspirations to swiftly build a strong connection.

A buddy who first shows you a lot of love and presents, making the friendship seem strong and encouraging.

The phase of Devaluation:

As the relationship develops, the narcissist shows their real colours by methodically undermining her self-worth by neglecting, humiliating, and criticizing her.

As an illustration:

A partner who progressively loses interest in you and starts criticizing your appearance, job, or friends drives you away from your support networks.

A coworker who gossips about you or takes credit for your accomplishments, undermining your efforts at work, creates a toxic work environment.

The phase of Discardment:

You may eventually be temporarily or permanently abandoned by the narcissist, which will leave you feeling bewildered, used, and emotionally destroyed.

As an illustration:

An abruptly ending relationship might leave you without closure and increase the emotional agony of the breakup by your spouse, possibly spreading unfavourable stories or expressing skewed opinions about you with friends and family.

A buddy who abruptly leaves your life and reappears only when they needs anything from you is taking advantage of your forgiveness and assistance.

PART THREE:

The Impact of Narcissism on Family Members:

Many of the negative effects of narcissism on family members are detrimental to the dynamics of the family as a whole. The list of particular effects of narcissism on family members follows.

Emotional Manipulation: Narcissists frequently use emotional manipulation to hold onto their position of authority and control within the family.

Family members may be subjected to guilt-tripping, emotional manipulation, and gaslighting.

Low Self-Esteem: Living with a narcissistic family member can hurt other family members' sense of value and self-worth.

They may always seek approval and recognition, but they rarely receive it.

Anxiety and Stress: Family members of narcissists may experience ongoing anxiety and stress as a result of their unpredictable and frequently volatile behaviour.

It becomes normal to steer clear of narcissists at all costs.

Isolation and Alienation: Narcissists have a tendency to distance their loved ones from their social circles, which makes it difficult for them to approach people for help or praise.

Family members may feel cut off from friends and other members of the extended family as a result of the narcissist's domination.

Role confusion: Roles may get skewed when a narcissistic individual lives in a household. Certain family members may be forced into caregiver or enabler roles, while others may be sidelined or used as scapegoats.

This role confusion could lead to a household with unclear roles and responsibilities.

Families of narcissistic individuals may be under continual pressure to accept, respect, and give them admiration.

Their mental well-being becomes reliant on the demands and emotions of the narcissist.

The narcissist's propensity to prioritize their own needs and desires over those of their family members can cause tension in relationships.

There may be sibling rivalry, marital problems, and parent-child conflicts.

Emotional Difficulty: To prevent an argument with the narcissist, family members may suppress their own emotions.

As a result, the family may find it difficult to talk and get their feelings out in healthy ways.

Effects on Children

Narcissistic parents can have a big influence on their children's development. Children may struggle with low self-worth, inferiority complexes, and a persistent need to win their parents' favour.

They might also acquire unhealthy coping mechanisms like people-pleasing or an overreliance on oneself.

Effect on well-being:

Diseases such as depression, anxiety, and physical discomfort can arise.

The Impact of Narcissism on Relationships:

Narcissism can greatly impact love and connections—in romantic relationships and inside the family. This is a detailed account of the ways that narcissism affects romance and relationships:

Lack of Empathy: Narcissists frequently struggle to understand and relate to their partner's needs and feelings because they lack empathy.

This lack of empathy could make the partner feel emotionally neglected and alone.

Need for Admiration: The insatiable desire for acceptance and respect drives narcissists. They might seek this acceptance elsewhere, which could lead to adultery or a focus on getting attention from people outside of the relationship.

Emotional Manipulation: Narcissistic individuals may employ emotional manipulation strategies to maintain control over their relationships. This could involve guilt-tripping, gaslighting, and emotional blackmail.

These manipulative strategies may leave partners feeling confused, uneasy, and trapped in the partnership.

Narcissists frequently become defensive when faced with criticism or other perceived challenges to their self-esteem. As a result, disagreements inside the partnership can get worse.

Partners may refrain from talking about important issues to prevent the narcissist's defensive reactions.

Unrealistic Expectations: Narcissists may expect their spouse to constantly fulfil their demands and wants, holding them to unreachable standards.

The partner may find it emotionally taxing and unworkable to fulfil these expectations.

As a result of feeling compelled to meet the narcissist's emotional demands, partners of narcissists may display codependent tendencies.

They may prioritize the narcissist's satisfaction over their own, which could be detrimental to their own emotional and mental health.

Low Self-Esteem in Partners: Poor self-esteem can arise when a partner in a relationship with a narcissist links their worth and self-esteem to the narcissist's acceptance.

They could frequently question their value and worth.

Isolation from Support Systems: Narcissists may isolate their partners from friends and family, which makes it harder for them to seek approval or support from those outside of the relationship.

This seclusion could make the victim feel even more dependent on the narcissist.

Effect on closeness: Narcissism may make it more difficult for a couple to be emotionally close. Partners may feel they are unable to be sincere or honest with a narcissist since they are solely focused on themselves.

Because a narcissist may prioritize their wants and performance over those of others, sexual connection may also suffer.

Difficulty Terminating the Relationship: Narcissists frequently employ manipulation and guilt-tripping as control tactics, which makes it challenging to end a relationship with them.

Out of obligation or fear of retaliation, one or both spouses may decide to keep in touch.

Relationships with narcissists can be challenging and emotionally taxing.

Ensuring the wellness of both parties frequently involves setting reasonable limits, attending therapy or counselling sessions (individually or in groups), and, in certain cases, deciding to end the relationship.

Chapter 5: Establishing Healthful Limits

Healthy relationships with those who suffer from narcissistic personality disorder require that limits be set. By establishing boundaries, you may defend yourself against the deceptive actions and emotional abuse of the narcissist. Preserving your dignity and self-respect enables you to set explicit boundaries and expectations for how you will be treated.

In narcissistic relationships, boundaries are crucial because they foster a secure environment where both partners may express themselves without worrying about criticism or coercion. You may also stop the narcissist from controlling the relationship by establishing boundaries, which will stop them from taking advantage of you. Setting boundaries also makes it more likely that the narcissist will respect your needs and emotions, which promotes better communication between the two of you.

It's crucial to keep in mind that establishing boundaries just refers to how much time and effort you are ready to invest in the relationship with a narcissist, not that you have to stop communicating with them completely. For setting boundaries to be successful, both sides must be patient, understanding, and communicative.

The following techniques can assist you in establishing and upholding boundaries with a narcissist:

Don't defend, rationalize, or explain oneself. It's crucial to avoid giving narcissists the satisfaction of an explanation since they frequently attempt to mislead their victims into feeling guilty or humiliated.

When it doesn't seem right, leave. Never be scared to leave a toxic relationship with a narcissist and put your own needs first.

Choose what you will and won't put up with. Recognize your boundaries and make sure the narcissist understands them.

Jot down the current events. If things go out of control later on, having a record of what transpired will help you remain composed and recall what happened.

Recognize that no matter what you do, some people will never respect your boundaries.

Establish Clear Boundaries For Yourself: Put your needs first by establishing boundaries you will abide by regardless of what the other person does or says.

Avoid arguing with narcissists: Narcissists tend to twist words and never own up to their mistakes, so it's better to avoid arguing with them whenever you can.

Communicate your needs and expectations.

Refrain from letting oneself be used or tricked.

Refrain from assuming accountability for the narcissist's emotions or actions.

Even if your thoughts and feelings diverge from the narcissist's, respect them nonetheless.

Establish and adhere to time limitations for your interactions with the narcissist.

Avoid arguing or debating with the narcissist; if needed, move on.

Don't allow the narcissist to steer the conversation; instead, pay attention to your needs and emotions.

Speak up if you feel mistreated or taken advantage of, and don't be scared, to be honest and open about your feelings without worrying about the narcissist passing judgment or criticizing you.

Refuse to yield to the narcissist's guilt-tripping strategies. Instead, remain resolute in your decision-making and resist the narcissist's use of emotional blackmail to gain what they want.

Prioritize self-care activities like exercise, meditation, writing, etc., to take care of yourself before taking care of others in your life, including the narcissistic person.

Feminine Narcissist in Secret

Although the covert narcissist doesn't openly declare her superiority, she will undermine others by spreading rumours and taunting them.

She can manipulate disorder to maintain her status as the centre of attention.

They are typically attracted to caregivers who can satiate their compulsive desire for attention. They may cause mayhem or a catastrophe if they believe they aren't receiving enough attention to ensure they do.

In addition to being a long-suffering victim, the covert narcissist saps the emotional stamina of everyone in her vicinity. With these kinds of narcissists, a state of narcissistic collapse is more apparent.

When someone has a narcissistic injury, you probably feel like you have to be cautious around them. This condition of affairs could be reached by the covert female narcissist following a setback of some kind. They will struggle to maintain their phoney persona and become hostile. This could occur, for instance, if they don't receive the desired employment offer if a family member declines to provide capital to their venture, or if anything else goes wrong and their plans fall through.

You might just get stonewalled if your narcissistic spouse starts crying or venting her frustrations on you without giving you a reason.

Anxiety and depression are also more common in veiled narcissists. They frequently exaggerate their ailments out of self-pity.

Techniques for Changing and Manipulating Their Victims

While not all narcissistic women behave in the same manner, there are many sorts of narcissists who employ distinct tactics to influence the people in their lives.

Techniques of Control Employed by the Hidden Female Narcissist

The following are some well-known strategies that the covert female narcissist may employ:

Gaslighting is a tactic they can employ to get you to doubt your perceptions and your account of what happened. If you confront them about something they did incorrectly, they will be particularly interested in this tactic, as they will wonder how you remembered it. They can claim that what you remember didn't happen, or they might even say you're going insane and have a psychological issue.

The triangulation tactic is another one that your covert narcissist could employ. She may introduce a third party into your relationship to cause conflict and disparage you in her conversation with them. She can also cast doubt on you by using this person's views.

Additionally, the subliminal female narcissist might reflect her flaws onto you. They frequently accuse their victims of actions they know they committed themselves. When someone holds the victim in a relationship responsible for all the issues, it also amounts to victim-blaming.

As a kind of punishment, they use the silence treatment to confuse and unnerve their victims. In addition, it's a control mechanism since the victim tries to appease the narcissist by trying to figure out what went wrong.

A subversive narcissist may also use the love bombing tactic to maintain control over their target. This can involve showing them a lot of care, compassion, and even gifts to win their love and trust. If you break up with her, she can also attempt to manipulate you by hoovering to get your attention again. This tactic is comparable to "love bombing". You might also receive many presents and praise. But it can also refer to actions considered "stalkerish," including liking your postings on social media if you are still friends with these people or even sending you presents. Examples of these behaviours include texting you all day long. Should they succeed, you'll find yourself drawn back into the partnership.

To discredit you, the covert narcissist may also employ a cruel tactic known as a smear campaign, in which they propagate lies among your friends, family, and even coworkers. She may disseminate false information in larger social circles, and this smear campaign could not be restricted to people close to you. Maybe you won't realize anything is wrong until you notice that people are avoiding touch with or ignoring you. If you disclose the abuse, you will be treated as the source of the issues. A narcissist who is losing power over you will attempt to manipulate how other people perceive you.

Those who are covert narcissists are particularly likely to launch a smear campaign following narcissistic damage. For instance, if you've broken up with them and stopped responding to their attempts at hoovering.

Recovering via Self-Acceptance: Accepting Your Whole Self

One of the most powerful healing tools we have in our fight against narcissistic abuse is self-acceptance. To recover completely, we must accept all aspects of who we are, flaws and all, past and present, successes and failures. True healing and personal development can result from this process of accepting who you are as you are, without condemnation or criticism.

Recognizing Your Acceptance

The goal of self-acceptance is to embrace and love the person you are right now. It entails embracing the past, owning up to your shortcomings, and appreciating your accomplishments. It's about accepting that you're not flawless and a work in progress. It's about learning to accept yourself for who you are and how you feel without seeking approval from other people.

To heal, self-acceptance is essential because it lets you go forward. You may acknowledge your past and experiences without allowing them to define you if you embrace them. You give yourself permission to move on from the past and find peace with it, which releases emotional energy so you can concentrate on the here and now.

Promoting Acceptance Of Oneself:

- Examine Your History: Examine your past experiences, accepting them as a necessary part of your life narrative, but do not allow them to define who you are or your prospects.
- Accept Imperfection: Recognize that everyone is fallible and has imperfections. It comes with being a human. Celebrate your individuality and see your flaws as opportunities for improvement rather than as reasons to criticize yourself.
- Forgive Yourself: Self-acceptance and self-love are demonstrated by the forgiveness of oneself. Let go of your shame or remorse for previous decisions

or mistakes. You did the best you could using what you knew and could at the time.

- Honor Your Strengths: Acknowledge and honour your advantages. Appreciate these traits, whether kindness, resiliency, creativity or something else entirely.

- Engage in Mindfulness Practices: Mindfulness entails accepting things as they are, judgment-free. It's an effective method for encouraging acceptance of oneself.

Chapter 2: The Landscape of Emotions

I find that navigating the emotional terrain of a narcissistic marriage is like setting out on a difficult journey through an unrelenting storm as I dig deeper into the complex web of emotions interwoven inside such a marriage. I will guide you in this chapter, illuminating the turbulent emotional terrain you might encounter.

Riding the Emotional Storm in a Narcissistic Marriage: Managing Your Emotions

As I describe the emotional voyage through a narcissistic marriage, it's critical to understand that these choppy waters can leave you feeling lost and confused. Permit me to guide you through the highs and lows of emotions that frequently characterize these kinds of partnerships, acting as your compass in this choppy sea.

Intense, conflicting, and overpowering feelings characterize the turbulent world of narcissism. Even in a relationship, you may vacillate between the opposed emotions of optimism and despair, love and contempt, and, ironically, a deep sensation of loneliness. Navigating your sentiments might be difficult during these intensely bewildering emotional whirlwinds.

Let's describe this emotional roller coaster in graphic detail: Imagine that one moment, your narcissistic partner shows you a great deal of love and appreciation. They have an enticing charisma that makes you feel like the centre of their universe. However, the mood changes in an instant. The admiration you once basked in is replaced with cold indifference or sharp criticism. It can be confusing to experience the emotional whiplash in these kinds of circumstances.

In this case, I can remember times when I doubted my sense of reality and sanity. Was the love I was feeling fake, or was it genuine? Was it something I did that caused this abrupt behaviour change? These are typical queries that come up when navigating the volatile emotional environment of a narcissistic partnership.

This is the fundamental reality: Your instability is not reflected in these emotional swings. They result from narcissism's erratic and unpredictable nature. Narcissists are skilled at controlling your emotions, and they frequently utilize their attractiveness to keep you under control. They can quickly switch from being kind to critical to preserve their power and throw you off emotionally.

Regaining emotional equilibrium starts with understanding your feelings in this situation. It's similar to being given a map to help you through dangerous terrain. You give yourself the power to take back control of your emotional reactions and navigate your way out of this emotional maze by admitting the emotional storm you're caught in.

It can be freeing to realize that these oscillations are not a result of your instability but rather a deliberate tactic used by the narcissist. It can assist you in taking back control of your emotional health and set off on the path to recovery and emotional independence.

The Cost to Self-Respect and Self-Esteem: Taking Care of the Emotional Storm

While I explore the horrifying effects of a narcissistic marriage on your sense of self-worth and self-esteem, please know that you are not travelling this path alone. As I offer these ideas, I hope many who have gone before you may find courage, comfort, and a glimmer of hope amid the storm.

Imagine a scenario in which your narcissistic partner continuously minimizes your accomplishments. Maybe you just got promoted at work, and instead of everyone applauding you, they make fun of you. They might say, "You only got that because of luck," which would doubt your achievement. These emotional jabs gradually eat away at your sense of who you are, much like unrelenting sea waves eroding the beach.

In a similar vein, your partner could be the one to undermine your self-assurance all the time. For instance, people can react sceptically if you say you want to follow a personal interest or objective, implying that you're incapable or that your aspirations are silly. Your confidence is gradually undermined in this way.

Then, there are the instances of excruciating criticism. Imagine that after you've finished a task or made a meal, you receive relentless criticism of your work. Every imperfection—actual or imagined—is brought to light and made larger. These critiques seem like an ongoing attack on your skills and value.

It's important to realize that this emotional deterioration is typical of narcissistic relationships as you go through it. Narcissists frequently get a warped sense of power by undermining other people. They feed off your weakness to protect their frail ego. However, it's critical to understand that your value is independent of your partner's thoughts or behaviour.

No matter how much you are denied validation, you are valuable. Like the seashore, your self-esteem may have deteriorated, yet beneath the surface remains your genuine self-worth, ready to be rediscovered and strengthened.

The first crucial step in restoring your self-esteem is realizing how much it has been damaged. It's similar to standing on the coast after a hurricane and assessing the harm the unrelenting waves have caused. Recognition is the first step toward recovery. Before you can heal the scars, you must first acknowledge them.

It takes self-compassion and self-discovery to rebuild your self-esteem. It entails learning to drown out the echoes of your partner's criticism and swap them out with positive reinforcement of your value. It means surrounding yourself with individuals who will encourage and affirm you and be pillars of strength on your journey toward healing.

Although this path might be difficult, it can also be incredibly transforming. As the beach gradually restores its lost sand, so do you have the inner fortitude to rebuild your self-worth. We will examine useful techniques for fostering self-worth, escaping the shackles of narcissistic invalidation, and emerging into the light of self-empowerment and healing as we proceed through the upcoming chapters.

Coping Techniques for Emotional Sturdiness: Getting Through the Storm

It's crucial to provide oneself with coping mechanisms for the never-ending emotional maelstrom that frequently accompanies a narcissistic marriage. These techniques are more than simply tools; they are lifelines that can help you navigate the turbulence and emerge from the storm stronger and more resilient than before.

Allow me to discuss a few of these essential coping techniques with you, as I have repeatedly found them to be effective means of fostering emotional resilience:

1. Establishing Limits: Imagine the following situation: your narcissistic partner is trying to control or manipulate your emotions or behaviours by pressing your emotional buttons. Establishing firm and unambiguous limits becomes your shield during these times. This entails authoritatively voicing your demands and boundaries and refusing to accept pressure or guilt. For example, you can politely say that it is inappropriate for your partner to minimize your accomplishments or make you feel insecure. If they continue, you may stop talking to them or ask a therapist or close friend for help.

Boundaries shield your mental well-being from an unrelenting emotional assault.

2. Developing Self-Compassion: Take a moment to picture yourself comforting a close friend experiencing a comparable emotional struggle. To them, what would you say? You would probably be kind, sympathetic, and understanding. Give yourself the same compassion now. Acknowledging that your feelings are appropriate and normal reactions to the difficulties you encounter is critical.

For instance, show yourself the compassion you would show a friend if you're feeling overtaken or offended by your partner's actions rather than criticizing yourself for being so open and vulnerable. Remind yourself that feeling the way you do is acceptable. Take part in soul-nourishing self-care activities, such as journaling to work through your feelings, finding inner peace via meditation, or spending time with loving, supporting people.

3. Seeking expert Support: When navigating the emotionally perilous seas of a narcissistic marriage, it is acceptable to seek expert help. Counsellors and therapists are qualified to offer you insightful advice and useful tools to help you develop emotional resilience.

Think of this as an analogy: the ship's captain in a storm at sea will frequently consult with knowledgeable navigators or specialists to determine the best course of action. Similarly, expert assistance can act as a compass for you while you seek emotional resilience, assisting you in navigating the challenging emotional terrain.

Emotional resilience is about owning your vulnerability and actively fostering your inner strength rather than stoically weathering the storm. It's the process of discovering how to flourish in the face of emotional upheaval, even in the raging oceans of narcissism, rather than merely get by.

In the upcoming chapters, we will explore these coping mechanisms in more detail, providing you with a complete arsenal for regaining your emotional health. You will find that you are stronger and wiser than you ever could have thought and that you can not only survive this emotional storm but also emerge into the sunshine of healing and freedom. Recall that you are naturally resilient enough to successfully negotiate this turbulent terrain.

Phases Of Drug Addiction

What would happen then if you were to get involved with a narcissist? Idealization, devaluation, discarding, and hoovering are the four main stages that these kinds of relationships frequently go through.

And going through these stages may feel like you're on a less-than-jovial merry-go-round. You feel like you've gone through a vintage washing machine wringer at the end of it all.

THEORIZATION

"Idealization," the initial stage of a narcissistic relationship, is arguably the most harmful. They lure you in like this!

This is the phase in which narcissists always enter into new relationships, and it's during this time that they will truly make you feel special.

This is the part where they show you all the love and appreciation they deserve while pretending to be the person you wish them to be. They typically possess a sixth sense of knowing what you want and are extremely bright.

During this phase, you can find that you can't get enough of this person.

Being with them is thrilling, and you might not think that you've found someone who is that "in touch" with you. It seems like you two have a great chemistry.

You might be pampered and nourished in amazing locations, taken on thrilling adventures, showered with beautiful gifts, and deluged with "love letters" telling you how precious and great you are. You will feel so good about yourself that you ignore some warning signs.

You might think this person is "the one" quite quickly! When you're with this ideal match, your boundaries and defences come down.

Because you're in their paws, you ignore any "red flags" that the narcissist may be showing you. Or, "Wow, that person must have damaged her." You could even do it yourself. "He may just have had a horrible day." "I must have misinterpreted."

The narcissist could not be interested in spending the rest of their life with you, even despite their polite behaviour.

However, some narcissists are honest when they tell you how wonderful you are and are not consciously aware of what they are doing, which is why they are so persuasive. The truth is, they are not infatuated with you.

All you're doing is playing with their "love script," which they've projected onto you.

In the relationship, you enter the devaluation phase, where they remove their mask and reveal more of who they are to you.

EVALUATION

The narcissist in your life will start to manipulate you when they've fully taken advantage of you.

It will begin modestly, perhaps concentrating on your closest friends and family.

They can even try to drive a wedge between you and your loved ones. This makes them more determined to get what they want and takes away a reliable sounding board with whom they may share their experiences.

You are now solely reliant on yourself for support. Divide and conquer, they say.

The narcissist will gradually become more deceitful, fabricate stories, and lie to you.

Along with making demands, they will verbally abuse and insult you, accuse, blame, shame, threaten, and guilt-trip you. They will also withhold things from you, such as money or affection.

They could start making fun of you in public to "put you in your place," undermine your confidence, and appear more powerful.

They could turn aggressive and furious to intimidate you into giving up. At worst, they might start abusing you brutally.

At this point, it's typical to keep apologizing and justifying the narcissist's behaviour. This is partially because you fell in love with them at the initial stage. Still, it's also a result of the fact that they will continue to incorporate love bombs into their abusive tactics to keep you on edge, perplexed, and invested. And it functions nearly every time!

You might even discover that you are happy to ignore any warning signs. Not only are we allowing the narcissist to minimize us, but we are also failing to value our internal GPS, which is screaming "danger!"

The narcissist's dishonest tactics, which are dysfunctional coping mechanisms (more on this later),

You can even find yourself living in a state of confusion as you start to question your sanity and identity.

You can think you're incapable of doing anything well and not good enough. Your confidence will be destroyed, and you'll have to tread carefully to appease the person who used to make you feel so special.

THROW AWAY

A narcissist never stops looking out for himself. It could have been the money, the status of dating you, or even the "chase" that initially drew them into your relationship.

You are not the "supply" the narcissist needs once they have drained you dry.

Alternatively, the rug you've pushed under all those warning flags will be pulled out from under you if you've compromised the narcissist's sense of false self in any way.

To feed their ego, you will be thrown away like a pair of old socks and replaced with a "better" model.

It's a double-edged sword if you can get out before this time. You will most likely incite their wrath and become a target that they want to destroy at all costs, even though you will be freed from their daily abuse. They might take a fresh interest in this. The "enemy" will have turned into you.

It is best if you can remove yourself from the narcissist in your life as soon as possible!

HOOVER

One of two things might happen after a narcissist has rejected you or has managed to end a relationship with them.

They might try to reintegrate you into their lives or choose to ignore you.

The narcissist may leave you alone if they know you have been seriously hurt and that their actions have caused you significant emotional anguish because they feel special and validated.

This is also the reason they'll take advantage of your kids fast to hurt you even more emotionally. Keep in mind that true narcissists lack empathy—even toward their children—and depend on approval from others to feel deserving.

The narcissist may use any means necessary to take back control of you if they are unhappy that you are experiencing enough pain to validate their superiority.

They won't hesitate to use defamatory language, yell, threaten, plead, make false promises, or even act as though they've admitted wrongdoing in the past.

They might ask others for help if they cannot persuade you to return.

This stage is like the stage of love-bombing, only with a hint of history.

Once they've drawn you back in, the abuse cycle restarts and the narcissist will immediately revert to the devaluation stage.

A narcissist is not going to change. They need a narcissistic supply to survive, and they will do everything in their power to obtain it.

Should you and your partner be parents, the narcissist's intention could not be to fully reintegrate you into their lives but rather to comfort you whenever they need something concerning the children. They will devalue and dump you once they've served their role. You might notice that they are exceptionally nice, cooperative, and talkative if they are asking for more time to spend with your kids and there is an upcoming court date.

But you know what happens just after court? You guessed it: diminish and dispose of.

Overview of Narcissistic Personality Disorder

Not every individual who irritates us suffers from a personality problem. Everybody makes mistakes, and keeping up positive connections is a continuous effort. Because of the human condition, life is a struggle worth taking on. Some argue that the term "narcissism" is overused and misused in today's society. I respond, maybe so, maybe not. There is nothing new about the fact that narcissism is the real plague of our day. Yes, long before our current civilization existed, the narcissistic pandemic was present and destroying the earth. Its grips only missed Noah and his family; we all know how that ended.

NPD is a personality disorder—exactly what it sounds like. This disease is dangerous and devastating to those who approach it. The only condition where the person with it does not require therapy, but those around them do is non-psychotic depression (NPD). Narcissistic abuse victims will soon find themselves in the hands of a counsellor or physician, taking antidepressants, being admitted to psychiatric hospitals, being homeless or incarcerated, or even dead. The narcissist, on the other hand, is comparable to a disgusting driver filled with wrath on the road, leaving a trail of destruction in the rearview mirror, all the while never getting a scratch on their vehicle. The narcissist is a skilled illusionist with the sinister ability to attack with ferocity in secret and appear innocent in public. To individuals who are unaware of NPD, nothing about a selfish person makes sense. The aims, talks, routines, mental processes, and interpersonal actions of a narcissist are perverted and dysfunctional. They refuse to look in the mirror under any circumstances and live in the darkness they have made for themselves. Every issue and disagreement is the result of someone else's fault. It takes practice to recognize the telltale signs of narcissism, and even then, a well-trained narcissist may fool even the most astute and intelligent people.

The world has transformed due to the internet in every manner possible, including in the realm of narcissism. Our only options for doing information research before the advent of Google and YouTube were libraries and bookstores. The only sources of information regarding the narcissistic personality back then were people working in the mental health area and others who had never personally felt its wrath. For the first time in history, the truth is being made public and allowed to spread, and this unrestricted access to knowledge is changing people's lives.

The first rule in handling a poisonous individual is to never label a narcissist as such. Resist the urge, no matter how much proof you have to support your position. If you do this, it could set off a boomerang effect in which the narc will automatically assume that you are the narcissist. The psychological game will pick up steam as soon as you prod a wasp colony while it's sleeping. By pointing out a narcissist, you give up the biggest secret in your armoury of protection: you are aware of their true nature and the tricks they are pulling. It is never good to divulge secrets; this is just another snare we must work to avoid. Once you know who you are dealing with, keep your thoughts to yourself and try to get out of the circumstance.

The absence of empathy lies at the heart of narcissism. Narcissists, to put it simply, don't give a damn. They don't just don't give a damn; they NEED to cause conflict to thrive. But protectiveness is a two-way street. It seems logical to think that everyone cares since we do. Although it seems inconceivable that other people could be so heartless and aloof, this oddity is evident. A narcissist's target will keep living in the same destructive cycles until they come to terms with this. No amount of willpower, empathy, tolerance, logic, affection, or time can make a narcissist change. Many have tried till the cows came home, only to find that there is never any progress in their relationship. The relationship with someone who does not care will always end, and frustration grows over time. It is unavoidable.

A narcissist may project an image of fearlessness, but this is a delusion, just like everything else about them is disordered. Selfishness is contradictory. Deep shame and insecurity are the foundation of NPD, but narcissists don't feel guilty or embarrassed when they take sweets from a newborn. They present a false front of perfection, encouraging others to aspire to be like them. The idea of being revealed is horrifying to a narcissist. But they dread not the shame of their actions but rather the loss of control. It's game over when the fake mask drops because that's when things always turn around. The narcissist's response is to promptly restore their fabricated persona and look for a fresh, gullible target to prey on. He or she cannot obtain supplies from anyone who can see past the mask. There is no going back for a victim once they see the true person. The dance is now underway. We can be set free by the truth.

In addition to being exposed, the narcissist fears abandonment greatly. Ironically, narcissists will cause this for themselves by estranging their targets once more. Because the empty spirit of a narcissist is rife with jealousy and incapable of sustaining inner peace and joy, it will take other people's prosperity and happiness. The narcissist needs this supply, or stolen positive energy, to survive. For a while, a narcissist can and will conceal their envy, but not indefinitely. The narcissist's constant mental tricks will eventually come undone, exposing the boiling hatred that serves as both their motivation and disguise. One of the worst setbacks for a narcissist is running out of supplies, although it occurs frequently. Maybe, just maybe, this is the inherent karma they are meant to go through.

Narcissistic Personality Disorder Causes

Among these are:

1. Early Life Events:

According to research, early life events may have an impact on the development of NPD. These experiences can include not having emotional support or validation as a child, having a loved one reject or criticize you, being abused or neglected, getting too much praise, growing up without limits and discipline, or having overly protective parents. Furthermore, traumatic experiences may also be relevant.

2. Genetics:

Given that NPD often runs in families, there may be a genetic component to it. Certain genes have been linked in studies to a higher risk of NPD and other psychiatric disorders. The risk of getting NPD may increase if certain genes are inherited from one or both parents. It's crucial to understand that while a family history of the illness may raise the risk of developing symptoms, it does not ensure that narcissism will manifest.

3. Environmental and Cultural Factors:

The development of certain personality traits, particularly those linked to NPD, can be influenced by the society in which an individual is raised. The emphasis on individualism, power, achievement, and self-importance in individualistic cultures may be a factor in the increased frequency of narcissistic tendencies. In contrast, collectivist cultures—that place a higher value on the needs of the collective than on the needs of the individual—tend to be less selfish.

4. Biochemical Elements:

There may be biological components to NPD. Furthermore, brain scans may indicate anatomical changes in NPD patients, such as decreased grey matter in brain regions linked to empathy, emotional control, and compassion.

Section Three

Narcissistic personality disorder (NPD) is not incurable, despite popular belief to the contrary. Change is possible, and everyone—including those with NPD—

can develop and grow. So why do so many individuals believe that psychotherapy is ineffective for treating NPD? The reason is that a large number of psychotherapy training programs focus on treating and advising patients with non-psychotic personality disorder. Rather than producing specialists, the majority of psychotherapy training programs aim to generate general interpreters. Learning this expertise requires at least three times as much advanced instruction as it is sensitive, valuable, and time-consuming. In addition, a lot of egoists steer clear of psychotherapy or end treatment early because they feel uncomfortable or fussed over. In conclusion, narcissistic personality disorder can be treated, but doing so calls for adherence to the prescribed course of action and technical training.

Do Therapists Help Narcissists?

Psychotherapy is undoubtedly a drawn-out and intricate procedure that frequently requires more time than most clients anticipate. Complete psychotherapy for Narcissistic Personality Disorder (NPD) might take up to ten years, and complex problems cannot be handled in ten sessions. Clients can halt the procedure at any time, a gradual process in stages.

Depending on the number of steps completed and the initial level of impairment, the therapy's effectiveness will vary.

Thus, what makes narcissists seek therapy? Usually, it's to deal with secondary stressors like work stress or strained relationships rather than to treat the main source of their NPD. In the end, therapy can be helpful for narcissists, but it's critical to keep in mind that it's a drawn-out and challenging procedure.

Options for therapy to address narcissism

Regarding recovery from Narcissistic Personality Disorder (NPD), there are numerous choices and strategies to consider. It's important to keep in mind that NPD can cause other problems, so it's advantageous to address these in treatment as well. Healing any underlying trauma and assisting the patient in understanding the coping strategies they have employed to deal with dysfunction and trauma are the two main objectives of treatment. Reversing maladaptive tendencies in NPD patients will probably require years of therapy.

Therapy for narcissism may have the following goals:

Identifying negative traits and behaviours that negatively impact life.

Investigating traumas that may have influenced one's behaviours.

Establishing emotional and interpersonal safety.

Focusing on the development of interpersonal skills.

Identifying and managing coping mechanisms.

Controlling self-talk.

Developing empathy.

Making an effort to show up authentically.

1. For narcissism, cognitive behavioural therapy

CBT, or cognitive behavioural therapy, combines behavioural and cognitive therapies. While behavioural therapy focuses on modifying negative thought patterns, cognitive therapy examines how research and beliefs influence an individual's behaviour and emotional state.

CBT is very beneficial for those who suffer from narcissistic personality disorder (NPD). Inaccurate and self-destructive ideas about oneself and others and deficiencies in certain skills that prevent individuals from adapting to change are characteristics of this condition. Thought-provoking and grounded in reality, CBT offers assignments that enable clients to immediately apply their learned skills. On the other hand, finding a skilled cognitive behavioural therapist or participating in a program that applies this remedy can help patients regain their internal balance and overall quality of life.

SET LIMITS WITH A CHILD WHO IS NARCISSISTIC

Setting up boundaries that are clear to a narcissistic youngster will help them understand boundaries and develop a feeling of responsibility. This chapter will cover the importance of boundaries and provide helpful advice on how to set and uphold them.

Boundaries serve as guidelines, outlining appropriate conduct and standards. They give our children a feeling of consistency, predictability, and security. Setting limits is crucial for narcissistic kids in particular, as they could find it difficult to identify them. Narcissistic kids usually rebel against or treat them disrespectfully when faced with limitations. They could act disruptively and get into arguments because they think the rules don't apply to them. However, establishing limits may give children the structure and guidance they desperately need.

Useful Methods for Determining Boundaries:

Consistency is crucial for setting and enforcing boundaries. Make sure that the penalties and rules are consistent to prevent misunderstandings.

When setting limits, explain to your child the rationale behind them so they may comprehend how these measures are meant to protect both them and other people.

When your child behaves appropriately, praise and reward them. Rewarding behaviour encourages people to abide by the rules.

Set limits based on the age and developmental stage of each child. Be mindful of your hopes and expectations.

Give your child some autonomy to help set some of the boundaries. They might develop a sense of accountability and ownership as a result.

Make it obvious what happens when someone crosses boundaries. Make sure the consequences fit the behaviour or deed and are pertinent.

When your child tests boundaries or challenges you, respond to them kindly but firmly. Steer clear of emotional and power confrontations.

Establish proper limits in your relationships and interactions. Youngsters learn knowledge through observation.

Include pictorial representations: Younger children can benefit from visual aids like charts and diagrams to better understand the concept of boundaries.

Limit your child's screen time and ensure the stuff they are exposed to aligns with the values of your home.

A sense of ownership can be instilled in your children by giving them age-appropriate duties and jobs. Children learn about their role in the home from this.

See a child psychotherapist or therapist if it becomes too difficult to set limits or if your child's behaviour is hurting others.

It may be challenging to set limits with a selfish child, but doing so is essential for their growth and your family's welfare. We'll continue to examine strategies for fostering a child's healthy and balanced development while navigating the challenges of raising a youngster with narcissistic tendencies in the upcoming chapters.

Chapter 14: Typical Behaviors of Narcissists in a Partnership

"Love does not pass away naturally. Frank Salvato once said, "Love must be killed, either by neglect or narcissism."

Depending on the type of conduct the other person in your relationship tends to display, you may simply determine whether or not they are a narcissist. Let's now examine a few indicators that can help you determine whether your companion is a narcissist or not. Even if a lot of the behaviours can point to NPD, a professional diagnosis can only be made.

They Make an Attempt to Win You Over

A narcissist can be quite charming and charismatic when they require something from you, as we well know. If you are in a relationship like this, they will make an effort to make you feel unique immediately. The idea is to gain your trust so you may lower your defences. A narcissistic partner will continue to lavish you with attention as long as you can fulfil their desire for you to serve them. They would go out of their way to make you feel like you were the centre of their universe. When someone tries to put you on a pedestal in the early stages of a relationship, you need to pay closer attention to their behaviour to ensure they are not acting sincerely.

They'll Dominate Discussions

The fact that narcissists like their perception by others is nothing new. As a result, they will never give up the opportunity to talk about themselves. The subject will undoubtedly flip to them the instant you try to talk to them, and that's all they'll be talking about. It's never a two-way conversation with a narcissist unless they want to control you. There will undoubtedly come a time when you cannot persuade the other person to share your opinions or feel the way you do. If you try to tell them a narrative about something that happened at work, for example, you will never finish it because they will start telling their own story much sooner than you finish yours. If you attempt to contribute to the debate in any way, all of your opinions and remarks will be promptly disregarded or corrected when they are unnecessary.

They Could Make You Feel Insignificant

When you are in a relationship with a narcissistic individual for a considerable amount of time, you will notice that their initial reaction in any disagreement will be to write you off in a way that will make you feel unworthy. You can feel dehumanized since they won't allow you to be criticized. We feel our viewpoint matters to the typical person when we disagree with them. That isn't the case with narcissists, though. Whatever positive traits you once possessed that a narcissist found endearing will quickly turn into liabilities in their perspective. A narcissist may even present themselves as a saint who tolerated all of your flaws.

They'll Make an Attempt to Mold You

When you enter a relationship, people may attempt—often unintentionally—to alter you in various ways. However, because they are dealing with a narcissistic mentality, they will intentionally try to alter you. Undoubtedly, the upcoming transition will not be beneficial. They'll make an effort to separate you. You may notice that you give in all the time. It is obvious to every onlooker that you are a puppet under their control. You'll eventually become an extension of your narcissistic partner and lose your personality in the process. It will be difficult for you to discover your true self even after ending such a relationship because the narcissist spent the whole time reinventing you.

They'll Disobey the Law

Every partnership has ground rules that both parties agree to abide by. However, a narcissist will disregard the ground rules established for the relationship without hesitation. The problem is that we sometimes find people who disobey the norms attractive because we regard them as "rebels," but we don't see that these are symptoms of narcissism. Relationship standards are undoubtedly broken by someone who doesn't hesitate to violate social norms because, to them, relationships are nothing more than social contracts. Suppose someone tries so hard to win you over, yet during the first few exchanges, you witness them ignoring traffic signals, cutting people off, giving bad recommendations, etc. In that case, you can be certain that they are inherently selfish.

They Display a Feeling of Ownership

A narcissist will make an effort to display entitlement for most of the partnership. They may first appear kind and giving in an attempt to entice you. After that, though, their attitude of entitlement is visible in the recesses of their consciousness. In addition to expecting you to prioritize them in your life, they will always want special treatment from you. The difference between what they deliver and what they anticipate will be noticeable. They will constantly strive to be your universe's centre.

They'll Be Feeling A Lot of Bad Things

Since all narcissists desire to be the focus of attention, they will attempt to play on negative feelings. When you enter a relationship with someone who has a narcissistic personality, they will become angry if you don't give in to all of their requests, if you try to be critical of them, or if you don't give them the attention they crave. To make you feel insecure, to gain control over you, or to catch your attention, the individual will manipulate you with rage, sadness, and other bad feelings. It is a sign of a weak ego if your partner becomes irrationally angry over trivial arguments or when you cannot offer them your whole attention. It is an obvious symptom of narcissism.

They'll make every effort to keep you alone.

You can tell when a narcissist is trying to subjugate you and take control of you because you have a strong support network in place to keep you safe. Isolating you is, therefore, one of the most frequent things they will attempt to do once they have finished pretending affectionate and earning some of your trust. They may advise you never to invite people along when you hang out. Someone like that won't hesitate to fabricate lies to isolate themselves from you and your network of support.

Indeed, a narcissist may even bring up past disagreements with friends or relatives in an attempt to make you feel more isolated from your network of support. If you eliminate your support network, they will have total authority over you. You won't even be able to compete with their deceptive strategies.

They're Going to Assign Blame

It may be considered among the most typical indicators that you are interacting with a narcissist. They refuse to acknowledge any of their transgressions. They will always find a way to make everything seem your fault, regardless of who is at fault. Even if they could have taken action to change the event's outcome, they won't hesitate to blame you if anything doesn't go according to plan. They will avoid any responsibility if you expect them to accept it. In the unlikely event that they move to resolve a disagreement in the relationship, they will always make it clear that you owe them.

When It's Convenient For Them, They Will Speak.

A narcissistic spouse will only communicate with you when it's convenient for them or when they feel like it. They would never inquire about your future goals or how you could collaborate to create the life you want. All they will do is boast about themselves and their achievements all the time. There is very little likelihood that they will express interest in you or inquire about anything in your life. Are you curious about what brings them joy? It originates from outside factors, such as money and professional status. You may wonder if they are capable of romantic love or any other kind of emotional connection. Before long, you won't be able to relate to them, and you'll miss their commitment to the relationship, something they will never have.

The Path Back to Wholeness

embracing change and realizing the need for personal development

This chapter is an important section of our in-depth investigation, in which we explore the significance of realizing the necessity of change and fully embracing the infinite possibilities of personal development. This chapter takes us on an in-depth journey that shows us the bright road to empathy. Get ready for an engaging and incredibly human journey as we explore the complex mazes of self-transformation and discover the sublime potential of personal development.

The Need for Reform: Accepting the Imperative

If you dare, picture a whisper that dances on the airy breeze, a mesmerizing call that echoes through the sacred passageways of your soul. It is the loud, indisputable cry for change—an awakening to the fact that change is desirable and a necessary aspect of our lives. Let's take a wonderful and participatory trip together as we explore the great distance that separates us and how important it is to recognize that change is necessary to foster the rich soil of empathy.

a. The Sounds Inside Taking Note of the Transformation's Stirrings

Take a moment to pause and welcome the symphony of soft murmurs that originate in your heart's core. Is it possible to identify the deep desire for development, the subtle nudges toward self-awareness, and the unwavering realization that change is not only deeply desired but also imperative? Accepting these gentle prods—the songs of self-awareness that come from deep inside and invite us to live a more empathic life—is the first step toward realizing that change is necessary. Let the wisdom that naturally emerges from this reflective conversation act as the cornerstone upon which the seeds of your personal development will grow.

b. Challenging the Uncomfortable: Traveling Outside of Comfort Zones

Beyond the comforts of our well-traveled routes, there is fertile soil where growth thrives. Are you ready to experience the thrilling discomfort of personal growth without fear? We can effect tremendous change by accessing the limitless potential of our inner courage. With steadfast resolve, let us set out on this daring adventure—leaping fearlessly into the unknown territories of self-discovery, where the very fabric of who we are experiences a profound transformation. Accept the obstacles you will inevitably face because they are treasured growth-promoting factors and holy sources of self-awareness.

The Way of Personal Development: Reviving the Inner Seed

Let's descend even farther into the ethereal depths of personal development—a breathtaking journey that brings us to the sunny shores of empathy. We tenderly tend to the germination of empathy in the rich soils of our hearts through this transforming journey. Take full advantage of this interactive investigation as we embark on a journey of self-transcendence and discover the incredible potential that lies dormant in the mysterious domains of personal development.

a. Fostering Curiosity: Adopting an Attitude of Lifelong Learning

Curiosity turns into the bright light that leads to personal development. Are you willing to develop an unquenchable need for wisdom, understanding, and knowledge? We can open the door to endless learning and unbounded personal growth by taking a broad-eyed wonder and an open-minded approach to life. Accept the power of curiosity; the blazing furnace keeps the flames of growth burning brightly, guiding us to the amazing places of empathy and the brightest horizons of our truest selves.

b. Adopting Resilience: Using Fortitude in the Face of Misfortune

Being resilient becomes our steadfast armour on our difficult journey toward self-improvement. Are you ready to rise to the occasion with elegance and steadfast determination despite overwhelming adversity? Every challenge we face becomes a priceless chance for development, self-awareness, and the radical reconfiguration of our compassionate nature. As we negotiate life's difficult turns and turns, let us embrace resilience, understanding that the crucible of hardship contains the transformational alchemy that moulds us into kind individuals who inspire change.

www.ingramcontent.com/pod-product-compliance
Lightning Source LLC
Chambersburg PA
CBHW052135110526
44591CB00012B/1737